CITY LIVING

APARTMENTS, LOFTS, STUDIOS, AND TOWNHOUSES

CITY LIVING

APARTMENTS, LOFTS, STUDIOS, AND TOWNHOUSES

FRANCESC ZAMORA MOLA

UNIVERSE

First published in the United States of America in 2017 by
Universe Publishing
A Division of Rizzoli International Publications, Inc.
300 Park Avenue South
New York, NY 10010
www.rizzoliusa.com

Originally published in Spain in 2017 by
booq publishing, S.L.
c/ València, 93, Pral. 1ª
08029 Barcelona, Spain

© 2017 **booq** publishing, S.L.

All rights reserved. No part of this book may be reproduced,
stored in a retrieval system, or transmitted, in any form or by
any means, electronic, mechanical, photocopying, recording,
or otherwise, without prior consent of the publishers.

2017 2018 2019 2020 / 10 9 8 7 6 5 4 3 2 1

ISBN 978-0-7893-3270-7

Library of Congress Control Number: 2017933348

Printed in Spain

Editorial coordination: Claudia Martínez Alonso
Art direction: Mireia Casanovas Soley
Editor: Francesc Zamora Mola
Texts: Francesc Zamora Mola, Irene Vidal Oliveras
Layout: Cristina Simó Perales

Front cover: © P. Wünstel

Facing the challenges that come with the shortage of vacant land in increasingly dense urban environments, as well as the high real estate prices, architects, developers, and builders are designing houses around the principles of density, efficiency, and flexibility. They aim to find creative building solutions that can improve the architectural quality of urban environments, while allowing city dwellers to live comfortably within a community, and at the same time affording them sanctuary in their homes.

Within an urban context, where finding an empty lot is rare and, consequently, outrageously expensive, the options for the development of new homes embrace existing buildings, whose original use isn't necessarily residential. Fortunately, local ordinances, when it comes to new developments, can allow the recycling of structures to accommodate much needed housing. This includes the design of single-family homes that benefit from the advantages of urban living and from the commodities of suburban life. As a result, the projects that include this building typology encompass home remodels and extensions, upgraded industrial structures, entire apartment buildings transformed into single–family homes, as well as new constructions.

The projects included in this book illustrate the relationship between the city and those who dwell within it; projects that are the reflection of the diversity, convenience, and complexity of urban environments. Cities are places of action, culture, and history, and in the best cases, the design of houses is impregnated with the vibrant magnetism that cities release.

Proximity to schools, green areas, shopping centers, and cultural attractions is an advantage that comes with city living, and often a priority for many urbanites. But such a central location comes also with limitations, as we can observe with many of the house projects in the book: small sites (Annandale House, pp. 190-199), poor sunlight exposure (Slim House, pp. 200-205), lack of contact with exterior surroundings (H24 House, pp. 40-45), and existing buildings requiring extensive work (House of Joyce & Jeroen, pp. 26-33). Other limitations come from local ordinances, which add to the complexity of building in urban environments made of different components, including buildings, streets, and public open spaces. On the other hand, these local ordinances are guidelines that monitor the works in order to protect the architectural integrity of a place, and to improve it in the best cases.

City Living features houses containing open plans where spaces flow into each other efficiently, connecting existing and new sections; homes that are filled with natural light and that are not hermetically sealed, but rather open to the outside. A natural touch, whether it's a front garden, a backyard, or an interior courtyard, attests to the need to establish a connection between the house and nature, while complementing the hard surfaces of the city.

One can learn from the house designs shown in this book that modern needs and lifestyle, as well as an adequate architectural language, create a scenario for the creation of homes that stand out for their strong identity as much as for their capacity to become part of an existing urban fabric.

City Center

City Outskirts

With green area

Single-story

Multistory

CHAMBORD RESIDENCE

NATUREHUMAINE
MONTREAL, CANADA
© ADRIEN WILLIAMS

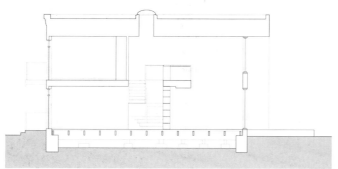

Longitudinal section

The second floor of this 1920s duplex was converted into three bedrooms and a study. The front facade was simply restored, but the back was completely transformed into a transparent area. Cantilevered over the backyard, the master bedroom is framed by the cedar wood used to trim the glass.

Color is used sparsely so as not to lose focus on the white and black color scheme accented by the light wood flooring, paneling, and furnishings. The splashes of color are playfully expanded by a mirror in the entry hall.

Custom-made, floor-to-ceiling cabinets are fully integrated into the design of the house. Careful detailing was put into aligning the cabinets with the seams between different flooring materials in order to demarcate specific areas.

A cedar-clad volume above the kitchen contains the master bedroom. It punches through the glass back facade, blurring the boundaries between interior and exterior, and cantilevers over the backyard, sheltering the patio below.

Also used on the exterior, the wood serves as a link between the two spaces, complementing the white and bringing warmth to the interior.

See-through elements such as open shelves and open riser stairs contribute to the diaphanous quality of the house interior, achieving constant visual and physical connections with the backyard.

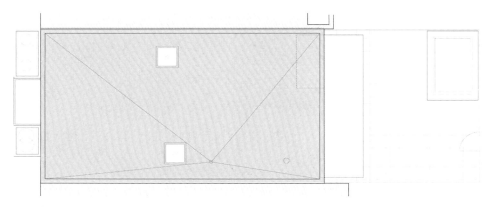

Roof plan

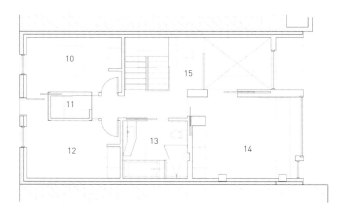

Second floor plan

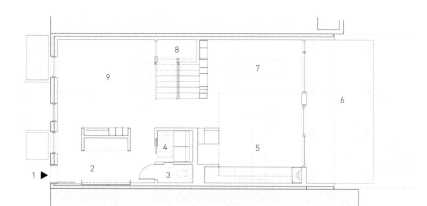

Ground floor plan

1. Entrance
2. Entrance
   vestibule
3. Bathroom
4. Laundry
5. Kitchen
6. Deck
7. Dining room

8. Storage
9. Living room
10. Bedroom
11. Walk-in closet
12. Bedroom
13. Bathroom
14. Master bedroom
15. Office

The bedroom on the second floor has openings along three of its four sides, creating visual links through the floor-to-ceiling windows with the exterior, through the door with the staircase, and through a sliding panel with the dining area on the ground floor.

BRISBANE STREET HOUSE

ALEXANDER &CO.
SYDNEY, AUSTRALIA
© MURRAY FREDERICKS

West elevation

East elevation

The aim was to reinvent a home for a young family, to create a space in which they could grow and explore. Although the site was compact, the space was fully utilized; in fact it was the limitations of the site that led to this simple architectural solution, based on a structure of beams and crossbeams. This formal balance is one of the great successes of the house.

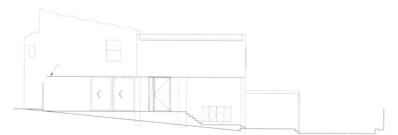

North elevation

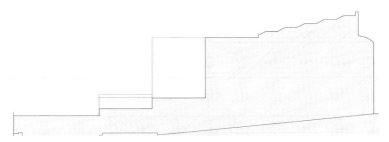

South elevation

The proportions of the site provided an opportunity to experiment with the scale of the kitchen; with a soaring fifteen-foot high ceiling, the room takes in plenty of natural light, reaching deep into the middle of the house.

White polyurethane cabinets, a stainless steel countertop, and Carrara marble backsplash contribute to the clean feel of the kitchen. This look is enhanced by the generous room proportions and the large openings that capture garden views.

Building section

1. Kitchen
2. Laundry
3. Storage
4. Dining
5. Living
6. Shower
7. Bathroom 1
8. Dressing room
9. Bedroom 1

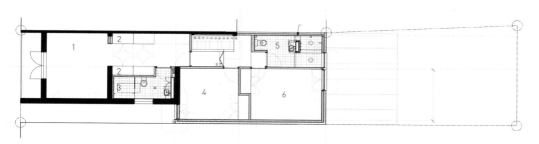

Second floor plan

1. Bedroom 1
2. Dressing room
3. En suite
4. Bedroom 2
5. Bathroom 1
6. Bedroom 3

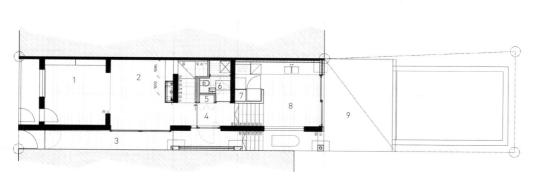

Ground floor plan

1. Living room
2. Dining room
3. Side deck
4. Entry
5. Storage
6. Laundry
7. Pantry
8. Kitchen
9. Deck

While maximizing the perception of space was a design priority, the use of materials set the tone, creating an airy and inviting feel throughout the house. Materials are beautiful and luxurious where they can be, but also resilient enough to contend with young children.

The bathroom has a Japanese style bathtub located behind the vanity. It is beautiful as well as practical, with white penny-round ceramic tiles (on the walls) providing a fun texture for the children.

HOUSE OF JOYCE & JEROEN

PERSONAL ARCHITECTURE
THE HAGUE, NETHERLANDS
© RENÉ DE WIT

Rear elevation

This house was designed for a young couple, Joyce and Jeroen. Initially the pair were only looking to bring the house up to date but they soon discovered that the structure was in much worse condition than it had appeared. Rather than seeing this as bad news, they took it as an opportunity to convert a typical Dutch house into a bright and contemporary dwelling.

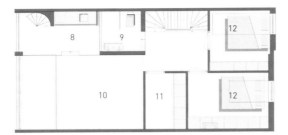

Third floor plan

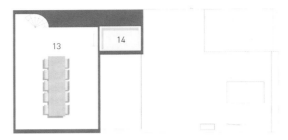

Roof floor plan

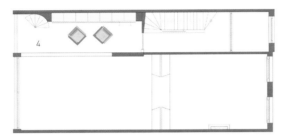

Mezzanine floor plan

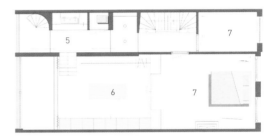

Second floor plan

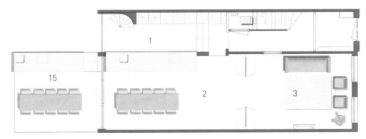

Ground floor plan

1. Kitchen	6. Wardrobe	11. Laundry room
2. Dining room	7. Bedroom	12. Guest room
3. Living room	8. Pantry	13. Roof terrace
4. Library	9. Bathroom	14. Jacuzzi
5. Bathroom	10. Workshop	15. Outdoor dining area

While the front facade maintains its classical flair, the house boasts a contemporary and sophisticated design that extends through the new, all glass back facade into a backyard.

The need of a thorough remodel led the owners and the architects to explore sensational design solutions. A vertical void in the interior, spanning over three floor levels, accentuates the full height of the typical row house.

Original elements such as old floorboards and a wood staircase are incorporated into the design. They contrast with new elements such as a spiral steel staircase, creating an interesting tension.

CUT AND FOLD HOUSE

ASHTON PORTER ARCHITECTS
LONDON, UNITED KINGDOM
© ANDY STAGG

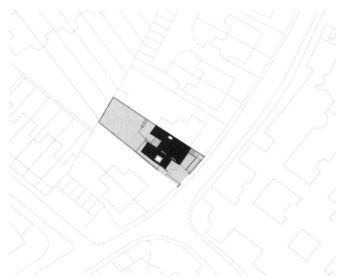

Location map

The remodel of an existing Victorian house includes a rear extension aimed at improving the connection between all interior spaces and between the house and the garden at the back of the property. The design is a juxtaposition of frames and squares of different materials. The use of stainless steel and glass gives the house a contemporary stamp and creates a marked contrast with the original brickwork.

Roof plan

Second floor plan

Ground floor plan

Basement floor plan

1. Garage
2. Dining
3. Kitchen
4. Bedroom
5. Living area
6. Study
7. Bathroom

The new front facade cantilevers from the original house over the garden to create a protected entry with a steel staircase, which connects the new living space to both the garden and the new kitchen and dining space below.

This glass-walled area articulates the existing building with the extension, connecting the different areas of the house and forming a link between the interior and the outside world.

The decoration, in simple lines and colors, uses only the most necessary elements, thus creating a clean and open interior space.

H24 HOUSE

R-ZERO STUDIO
MEXICO CITY, MEXICO
© AKI ITAMI

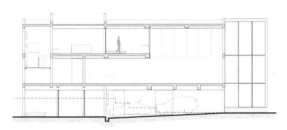

Building section

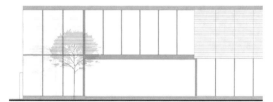

Main elevation

This family home situated south of Mexico City suffered from a lack of contact with its greater surroundings, so a unique landscape was configured around it. Thus, an intimate and private home was created. It appears to have been inserted into the city to form a part of its very fabric. Lightness and transparency dominate the home and lead the flow of interior movement.

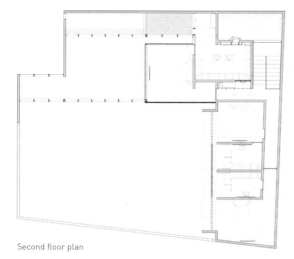

Second floor plan

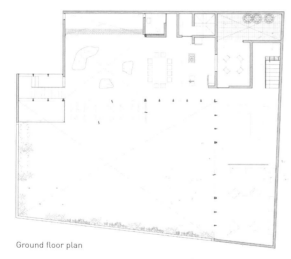

Ground floor plan

The property opens in an L shape toward the garden, a space in which the house is able to breathe. Despite the house's urban setting, the garden creates its own little oasis within it.

The size of the building seems to diminish as we move inside, from the entrance that's open to the expansive sky overhead, to the cozy privacy of the bedrooms.

Concrete blocks are turned into light fixtures, rising like a constellation to draw the night sky into the interior of the house.

BROWN VUJCICH HOUSE

**PETE BOSSLEY, ANDREA BELL, DON MCKENZIE,
KAREN NGAN KEE/BOSSLEY ARCHITECTS**
AUCKLAND, NEW ZEALAND
© PATRICK REYNOLDS

Located on a sloping plot in the heart of Herne Bay, this long and narrow house adapts to the incline of the ground. The property is accessed via a bridge over a planted moat. The entrance, a large, translucent glass wall, provides privacy while ensuring that a warm and gentle light permeates the interior.

West elevation

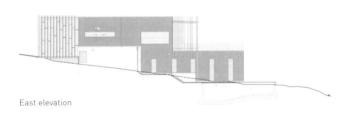

East elevation

Fine vertical cedar shiplap and double skin bagged brick reflect the clients' love for 1950s and 1960s architecture. The house is laid out so that it opens to the surrounding space, with a terrace and outdoor area for each room.

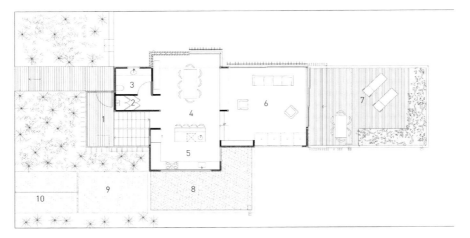

Entry level floor plan

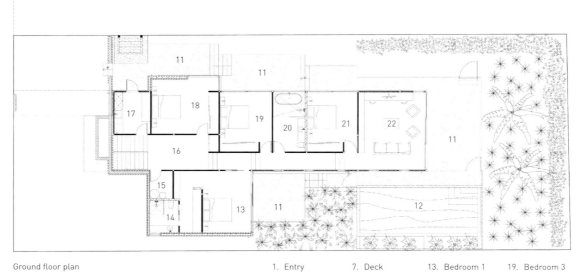

Ground floor plan

1. Entry
2. Cupboard
3. Powder room
4. Dining
5. Kitchen
6. Living

7. Deck
8. Roof
9. Parking area
10. Driveway
11. Terrace
12. Pool

13. Bedroom 1
14. En suite
15. Storage
16. Lobby
17. Laundry
18. Bedroom 2

19. Bedroom 3
20. Bathroom
21. Bedroom 4
22. Living room

On the upper floors of the house, vertical cedar and aluminum panels are used to modulate the degree of light and privacy required.

Playful colors, finishes, and hoop pine cabinetry combine with the clients' fantastic collection of 1950s-60s furniture, art, and ceramics to enliven the interior spaces.

An open riser jarrah wood and steel staircase features a stainless steel mesh guardrail that juxtaposes the rough brick wall. The use of elegant materials and rich textures throughout the house is enhanced by the soft natural light that filters through the translucent glass.

HOUSE IN HAMADERA PARK

AKIYOSHI NAKAO/COO PLANNING
SAKAI, JAPAN
© EIJI TOMITA

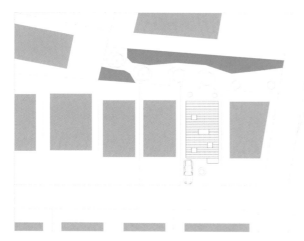

Location map

Seen from the outside, this family house in a residential area of the Japanese city of Sakai looks like a typical Japanese home, but its interior recreates the feel of a Parisian apartment. The rooms, paneled entirely in wood, have a cozy feel. The owners' extensive book collection is displayed along the length of several walls.

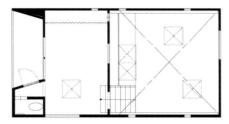

Second mezzanine floor plan

Roof plan

Ground floor plan

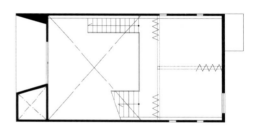

First mezzanine floor plan

Given the location of the house in a dense urban setting, small windows and various skylights were strategically placed to bring as much light into the interior as possible, while maintaining privacy.

Height plays an important role in this design because of the narrowness of the plan. Nonetheless, the creation of mezzanine levels gives a feeling of wide, open space.

Both sidewalls are lined with bookshelves to maximize storage and keep the space clear of any obstructive furniture. The bookshelf that spans the full height of the space enhances verticality. In all, the house feels spacious and airy.

The openings cut into the wood surfaces resemble entrances to a cave; their rounded shapes highlight the organic look of the interior.

PÜNKTCHEN HOUSE

BRAUN & GÜTH ARCHITEKTEN - DYNAMO STUDIO
FRANKFURT, GERMANY
© P. WÜNSTEL

Section

This nineteenth-century house had been consigned to anonymity as a result of its post-Second World War renovations. It did, however, have some unique qualities that were deemed worth rescuing with renovation. The aim was not to create a contrast between old and new, but rather to integrate both visions and bring together the two eras.

The classic street facade features massive horizontal sandstone pieces, which are softened by dotted surfaces forming patterns in a textile-like way. The massiveness of the front facade contrasts with the lightness of the back wall, which opens the house up to the garden.

Cutting-edge computer technology was used to create the floral pattern of the window screens on the front facade. These screens—made of a felt-like material—slide behind oak shutters to expose the deep-set windows.

The interior design applies a limited and rigorous selection of materials combining existing and new elements to achieve a harmonious and comfortable atmosphere.

Colors were carefully chosen to create the desired atmosphere: dark, rich tones for rooms where one wants to spend quiet moments, and lighter colors to optimize light. Either way, the rich figuring of the wood flooring and furnishings complements both design choices.

The interior design is inspired by the music of José González. The shapes and materials echo the recurring sounds of his minimalist melodies.

Wood is used throughout as a unifying material, set against decorative wallpapers and bold
colors. This combination juxtaposes the natural
tones of the wood, which give the house a rustic
flair, and the lavishly patterned and colored walls,
which add elegance and zest.

Is there anything more inviting for a child than
a bed in a cave? This half-wood and half-purple
bedroom is both a refuge and a play room.

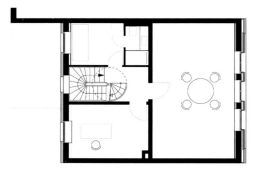

Attic floor plan

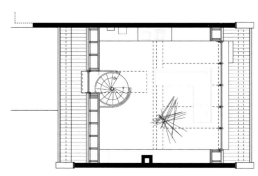

Fourth floor plan

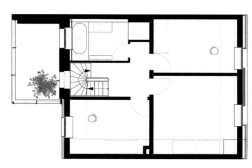

Third floor plan

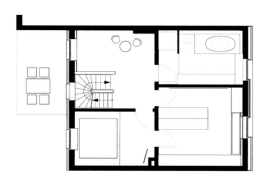

Second floor plan

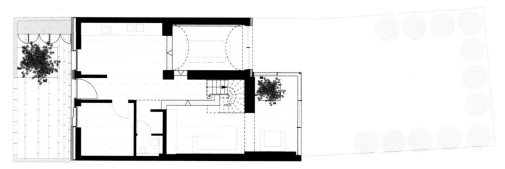

Ground floor plan

The cushions and giant Mikado design add a playful touch to this glass-roofed attic. Bright and balanced, it seems to have been designed to make one forget the world.

CAMELIA COTTAGE

KEVIN HUI/4SITE ARCHITECTURE
MELBOURNE, AUSTRALIA
© KEVIN HUI

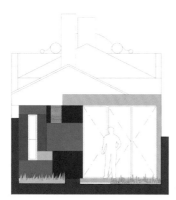

Rear elevation

B efore it was remodeled, this house comprised a series of additions that had been made over the years, which lacked both planning and light. In order to keep work to a minimum, it was decided to retain the existing bathroom. This unusual colored cubicle stands out over the monotone horizon of the urban landscape and has become an identifying feature of the construction.

The courtyard is connected to the house via the dining room: a place which, thanks to its views, is not simply a place to eat but also a place for settling down to relax with a good book.

The wall of the existing bathroom, with its cool colors, is the key to this house, connecting the interior to the outside.

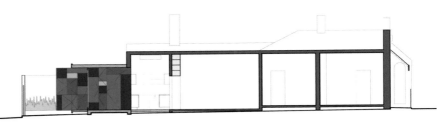

Building section

Floor plan

HOUSE IN SANBONMATSU

HIRONAKA OGAWA/HIRONAKA OGAWA & ASSOCIATES
KAGAWA, JAPAN
© DAICI ANO

This home is based on a simple idea, hiding a grand discovery beyond: a hipped roof with center cut, within which a courtyard is hidden right in the heart of the home. The opening lets light and wind into the property, brings a sense of balance to the exterior, and softens its relationship with the neighboring houses.

Site plan

The pitch of the roof and its changing forms gen-
erate different dimensions, which in turn provide
diverse views to the surrounding area.

North elevation

East elevation

South elevation

West elevation

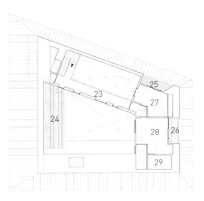

Second floor plan

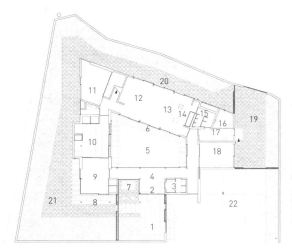

Ground floor plan

1. Entryway
2. Entrance
3. Storage
4. Hall
5. Courtyard
6. Terrace
7. Courtyard
8. Terrace
9. Guestroom
10. Japanese-style room
11. Main bedroom
12. Living
13. Dining
14. Kitchen
15. Storage
16. Bathroom
17. Lavatory
18. Reception area
19. Courtyard
20. Courtyard
21. Courtyard
22. Parking
23. Connecting corridor
24. Terrace
25. Terrace
26. Terrace
27. Bedroom
28. Bedroom
29. Storage

Terraces and gardens surround the building, softening the harshness of its geometric expression, while a small courtyard is framed in glass with most rooms arranged around it.

Sunlight floods this house, not just because of the garden that surrounds it, but also thanks to the interior patio around which it is set. The result is an open and well-balanced environment.

SINGLE FAMILY HOUSE

BECKMANN-N'THÉPÉ ARCHITECTES
PARIS, FRANCE
© OLIVIER AMSELLEM

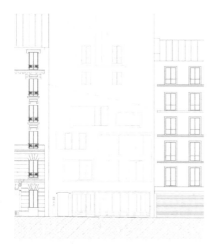

Street elevation

Sitting on a small plot and with the neighboring houses measuring on average 69 feet high, this home feels very hemmed in. Some of the best architectural solutions are born from limitations such as these, creating great design statements: a funnel-shaped courtyard to maximize light, or oblique walls to temper the feeling of seclusion.

The putty-colored concrete, which covers the house from ground to roof, echoes the other houses on the street. This facilitates its integration with the surrounding buildings.

The striking geometry of the building generates complex interior spaces full of character. Glazed surfaces are a key component of the design that allow a full appreciation of the geometry.

The architectural solutions of the exterior are matched inside: the walls are cut at different angles, transforming the space into a giant jigsaw.

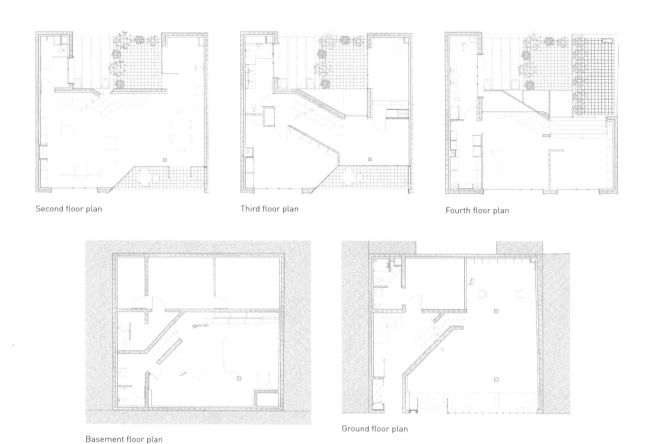

Second floor plan

Third floor plan

Fourth floor plan

Basement floor plan

Ground floor plan

The spatial experience is enhanced by the light that enters the building from different angles, creating subtle color nuances and a suggestive play of light and shadow.

The deep courtyard funnels the light into the rooms around it through large windows and skylights. The angular geometry of the building offers opportunities for slanted glazed surfaces that capture maximum light.

JAREGO HOUSE

CVDB ARQUITECTOS
CARTAXO, PORTUGAL
© FERNANDO GUERRA/FG + SG

Location map

This two-story house is presented as a white unit over a transparent ground floor and is structured around a central courtyard. The project explores the length of the building through a longitudinal axis, which emphasizes the visual relationship between the inside of the house and the garden. A white wall encircles the entire property, mirroring the main circular axis.

West elevation

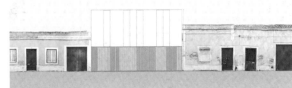

East elevation

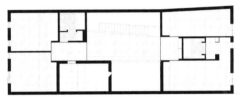

Second floor plan

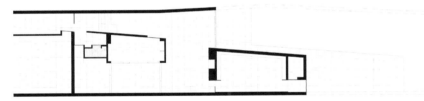

Ground floor plan

The exterior of the building appears as a skin splitting to reveal another layer. While the exterior skin is solid and white, this second layer is dark and considerably transparent. Large windows emphasize the relationship between the interior spaces, the garden, and the courtyard.

The design of the house explores the manipulation of natural light and its effect on different materials. In this respect, light guides our perception of materials and spaces, sometimes turning their mass and weight into lightness.

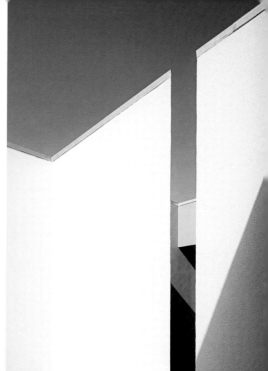

Light is carried from the courtyard to the common areas of the ground floor and to the first floor games room via a large glass wall that connects the house vertically.

RESIDENCE AND ARTIST STUDIO

CALIPER STUDIO
NEW YORK CITY, NEW YORK
© TY COLE

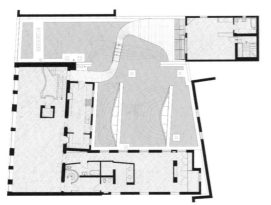

Floor plan

Artist Roy Lichtenstein had a series of buildings, built originally as a garage and metal shop, transformed into his home and workshop. A recent renovation of these spaces involved the creation of a new sculpture garden connecting the second floor of the existing buildings and the upgrade of a guest apartment and penthouse office.

The sculpture garden is actually a green roof above the artist's studio. The green surface splits and rises over two skylights shaped like eyebrows. Designed to regulate light, the skylights' complex geometry was achieved using cutting-edge technologies.

The sculpture garden is part of the effort to ensure the longevity of the existing facilities once used by Roy Lichtenstein. Not only is this very distinct project respectful to the original structures, but also enhances their original character by means of careful detailing and references to the aesthetic expression of the artist.

While the preservation of the artist's studio was a primary design objective, the project incorporated elements that improved the functionality and accessibility of the buildings.

OVAL HOUSE

ELÍAS RIZO ARQUITECTOS
ZAPOPAN, MEXICO
© MARCOS GARCÍA

This project presented a challenge that is increasingly common in Mexican architecture: the need to construct a house within a closed community that imposes aesthetic restrictions upon the buildings. Privacy was one of the primary objectives of the project. It was important to build a house that was secluded from the street, while also allowing plenty of natural light to enter.

What might at first appear to be a simple geometric composition is in fact revealed as a house that features great attention to detail: the delicate entrance gate is a good example.

The front facade, which faces the street, is tightly closed, while the rear opens up to the garden: the former protects the house while the latter enables it to breathe.

Ground floor plan

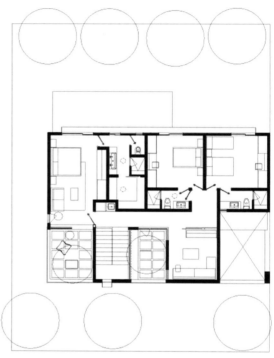

Second floor plan

Concrete, wood, and stone are the primary materials used in the interior, and are largely responsible for the feeling of austerity that governs the space.

BRISE SOLEIL HOUSE

SHAUN CARTER, PATRICK FITZGERALD/
CARTERWILLIAMSON ARCHITECTS
SYDNEY, AUSTRALIA
© BRETT BOARDMAN

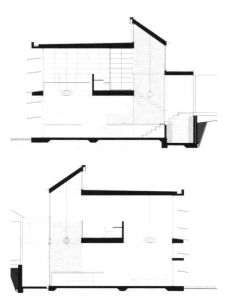

Building sections

The rear facade, which gives the house its name, features shading elements, which filter the light and heat of the sun. The property was built adjacent to a small house that dates back to 1860. Light and bright, the new building contrasts with the original structure. A patio connects the two buildings, forming a transition between old and new.

The shading elements of the rear facade create constantly changing light and shadow patterns on the interior surfaces throughout the days and the seasons, enriching the spatial quality of the room.

A double height space demarcates the kitchen and dining areas. This distinction enhances the open character of the space and gives it a vertical dimension.

The design boasts long sightlines that enhance the openness of the house interior and visually connects the interior and exterior, as well as the front and back of the building.

Upstairs, the library is organized around the opening in the floor, which enhances the light and creates a feeling of spaciousness for work and study.

TUSCULUM STREET RESIDENCE

SMART DESIGN STUDIO
SYDNEY, AUSTRALIA
© SHARRIN REES

Front elevation

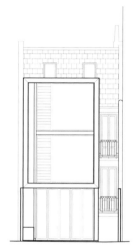

Rear elevation

When the plans were drawn up for the renovation and enlargement of this three-story townhouse in a residential neighborhood of Sydney, a spiral staircase formed a key supporting element. This sophisticated stairway unites the old and new sections of the house, enabling movement between the two while ensuring they retain their privacy.

The intense red of the walls, the carpet, the cream-colored chairs and the books on display lend this room an elegant yet comfortable air.

The travertine flooring and island and the white Corian® countertop add to the charm of the kitchen and allow light to extend throughout the room.

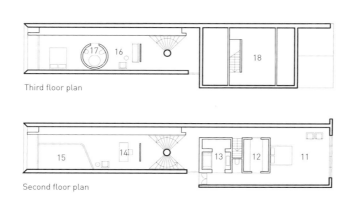

Third floor plan

Second floor plan

Ground floor plan

1. Forecourt
2. Porch
3. Formal lounge
4. Dining
5. Entry hall
6. Powder room
7. Living
8. Dining
9. Kitchen
10. Rear garden
11. Master bedroom
12. Dressing room
13. En suite bathroom
14. Study
15. Void
16. Guest bedroom
17. Bathroom
18. Attic

The staircase practically spans the width of the building and winds its way past six split-levels. The staircase was conceived as a central element that knits together the contemporary addition and the formal existing section of the dwelling.

In these bathrooms, dim lighting creates a sophisticated look. Despite its coolness, the texture
and shine of the marble provides a classic and elegant air.

The understated design, powerful forms, and exquisite detail that characterize this house are complemented by finishes that are elegant in a minimal-classical style.

EAST MELBOURNE HOUSE

ZOË GEYER/ZGA
MELBOURNE, AUSTRALIA
© DIANNA SNAPE

Remodeling this 1886 house brought it back to life, injecting it with dynamism and modernity. Now, its contemporary style embraces the traces of times gone by and creates a dialogue between the architecture of its past and the design of its present. This four-story property with two staircases is a true reflection of its owners' passion for art and design.

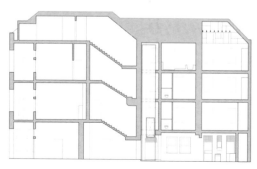

Building section after alterations and additions

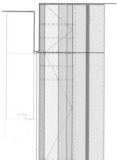

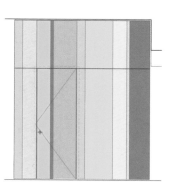

Hall paneling color options

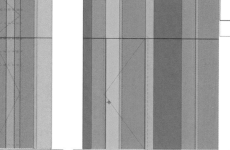

Hall paneling color options

The house's bathrooms and powder rooms are concentrated at the rear wing of the house. Access to these utilitarian rooms is through a colorful wall paneling and hidden door system. Nicely detailed sliding doors split all the upper floors to provide privacy between the rooms at the front and those at the rear.

Arches are one of the leitmotifs of this construction. Elegant and stately, passing through them brings us closer to the origins of the house.

The remodel preserves the original character of the house, while adapting it to the needs of contemporary living. The kitchen is made up of two adjacent spaces: a section fitted for entertaining and a section equipped for cooking.

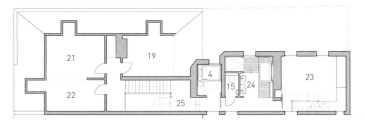

Fourth floor plan

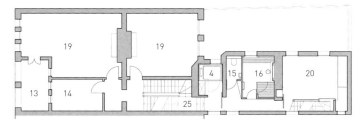

Third floor plan

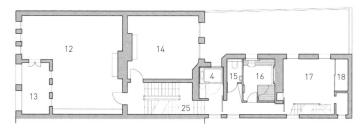

Second floor plan

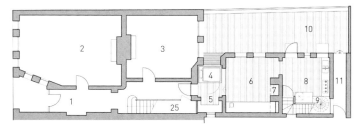

Ground floor plan

1. Entry
2. Sitting room
3. Dining room
4. Elevator
5. Elevator landing / Bar
6. Kitchen south
   (family kitchen)
7. Sculpture niche
   (old chimney)
8. Kitchen north
   (prep kitchen)
9. Stairs to cellar
10. Courtyard
11. Side entry
12. Library lounge
13. Balcony
14. Study
15. Powder room
16. Bathroom
17. Utility room
18. Laundry
19. Bedroom
20. Dressing room
21. Studio
22. Storage
23. Master bedroom
24. En suite
25. Stairwell

The design manages to bring out the cozy character of the house despite its very large size. The building was originally built to accommodate apartments, and then was turned into three separate dwellings. Its transformations had been possible only because the architects who designed it in the beginning took into account flexibility in the planning.

The gable roof has skylights that filter the sunlight. Together with the windows, they form the nexus between the house and the city.

The bathrooms boast striking designs. Some of them feature fireplaces, artwork, timber benches and glazed shower enclosures. Everything was built with attention to detail in a dialogue between bold colors and rich materiality.

STACKED HOUSE

NATUREHUMAINE
MONTREAL, CANADA
© ADRIEN WILLIAMS

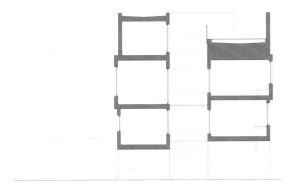

Longitudinal section

This project was carried out in collaboration with the owner, who wanted to play a part in the construction of his own house. The exterior design, in "patchwork" style, reflects the urban landscape of the Plateau district. A vertical construction was necessary due to the constraints of the plot: four boxes of different materials are stacked one on top of another.

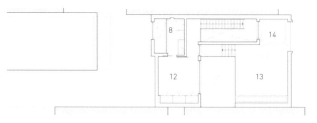

Fourth floor plan

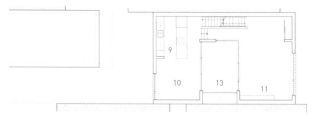

Third floor plan

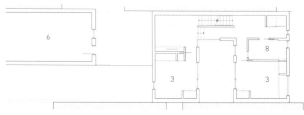

Second floor plan

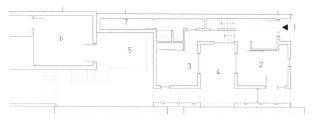

Ground floor plan

1. Entrance
2. Workshop
3. Bedroom
4. Interior courtyard
5. Neighbor's deck
6. Neighbor's residence
7. Walk-in closet
8. Bathroom
9. Kitchen
10. Dining room
11. Family room
12. Master bedroom
13. Terrace
14. Hot tub

The outer geometry is inspired by the house's surroundings and is in turn reflected inside. The design of the shelving unit in the lounge is a good example of this.

Inserting an empty space in the center of the house acts as a source of light and ventilation and also creates a small, private patio area.

- Bananes
- œuf
- lait
- café
- Konfiture

The kitchen is compact and functional with just a single bank of cabinets and a countertop along one wall and an island. Despite its narrow shape, it doesn't feel confined thanks to the skylight above the sink, and to the glass sliding doors that open to the courtyard.

The light grey hue of the tiles, the soft light, and the translucent materials are ideally suited to the bathroom, creating a relaxing atmosphere.

The house interior has references to Mondrian's neo-plasticism: Reduced form and material minimalism create a strong spatial expression that focuses on flowing circulation and uninterrupted sightlines. Black lines and primary colors are integrated in an asymmetrical way, yet, they create balance and harmony.

ARMADALE RESIDENCE

MADE BY COHEN AND ROBSON RAK ARCHITECTS
MELBOURNE, AUSTRALIA
© SHANNON MCGRATH

The transformation of what was a small, dark Victorian house into a refined and light-filled residence was based on a single premise: simplicity. The aim was to create an environment in which to unwind from the hustle and bustle of the city. To achieve this, a spacious and balanced interior was designed, an oasis in which every detail, subtle and overt, contributes to the harmony of the room.

A glass wall enhances the open plan living area and visually extends it to the patio. Its slender steel frames offer minimal obstruction to sight-lines, while blurring the boundaries between the interior and the exterior.

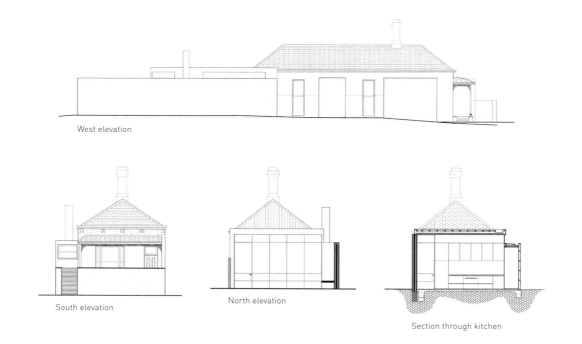

West elevation

South elevation

North elevation

Section through kitchen

Floor plan

1. Entry / Hallway
2. Master bedroom
3. En suite
4. Bedroom
5. Bathroom / Laundry
6. Study
7. Kitchen / Living area
8. Courtyard

Colors and finishes have much to do with the character of a space. The wood and white lacquer make this kitchen a cool, yet inviting space.

The house boasts a contemporary interior that focuses on comfort and functionality. A timeless decor is achieved through the use of honest materials, clean lines, and neutral colors.

THE LIGHTHOUSE 65

ANDY RAMUS, STEPHEN OSBORN/AR DESIGN STUDIO
FAREHAM, UNITED KINGDOM
© MARTIN GARDNER

Two neighboring buildings and an eight-foot-high embankment on its northern flank frame this waterfront home on the south coast of England. The property is accessed via the roof, through a glass cube that functions as a lighthouse. At night it lights up green when the weather conditions are good, and when the atmospheric pressure drops it lights up red.

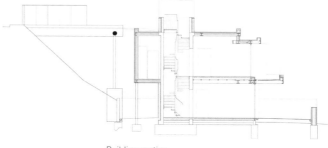

Building section

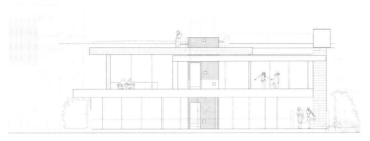

South elevation

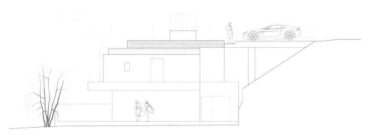

East elevation

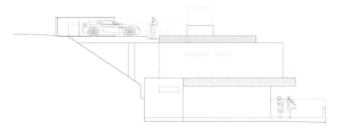

West elevation

The roof of the house, which sits 23 feet below street level, serves as a parking deck for three cars. The floor decks cantilever out from a central concrete core to create deep overhangs protecting the outdoor areas on the lowest floor.

The main rooms of this geometric construction face the sea, while the service areas are located to the rear of the house.

The design of the house maximizes the width of the property and allows unobstructed views to the sea through large sliding glass doors, and a glass guardrail.

The house is organized around a central concrete core that pierces the roof. At this level, it turns into a glass box that provides access to the house and acts as a lighthouse.

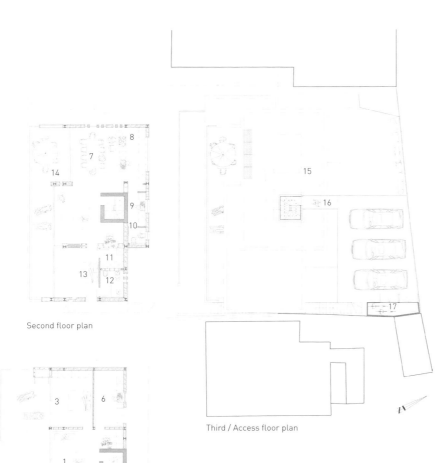

Second floor plan

Third / Access floor plan

Ground floor plan

1. Garden lounge
2. Patio
3. Bedroom
4. Bedroom
5. Bathroom
6. Storage / Utility

7. Dining
8. Kitchen
9. Utility
10. Washer / Dryer
11. Dressing room
12. En suite

13. Master bedroom
14. Balcony
15. Grass roof
16. Bridge
17. Bike storage

Thanks to the sliding glass doors, the bedroom is completely open to the outside, allowing the sunlight and sea air to pour in.

ANNANDALE HOUSE

CO-AP – COLLABORATIVE ARCHITECTURE PRACTICE
SYDNEY, AUSTRALIA
© ROSS HONEYSETT

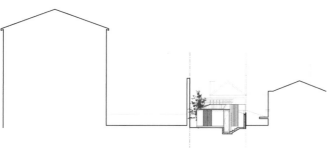

West elevation

The construction plot, which was exceptionally long and narrow, was a major factor in the remodeling of this two-story Victorian house. Given the nature of the site, enlargements were made at the back of the terrace and along the length of the house, creating a succession of separate levels and small patios.

During the winter, the glass balcony facing the courtyard captures the sunlight and becomes a source of radiant heat for the entire house.

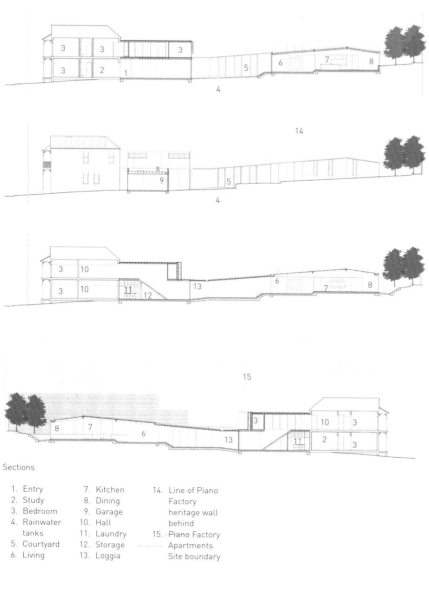

Sections

1. Entry	7. Kitchen	14. Line of Piano
2. Study	8. Dining	Factory
3. Bedroom	9. Garage	heritage wall
4. Rainwater	10. Hall	behind
tanks	11. Laundry	15. Piano Factory
5. Courtyard	12. Storage	Apartments
6. Living	13. Loggia	Site boundary

The site is bounded on its two long sides by taller structures—another single-family house on one side and an old factory converted into an apartment building on the other. This offered the opportunity to explore the use of glazed surfaces.

The extension, which was built along one side of the site at the back of the property, generates pocket courtyards. The result is a series of interior and exterior spaces at different levels, adapting to the slight slope of the terrain.

In addition to the many windows and glass balconies, skylights along the south side of the house capture the sunlight all year round.

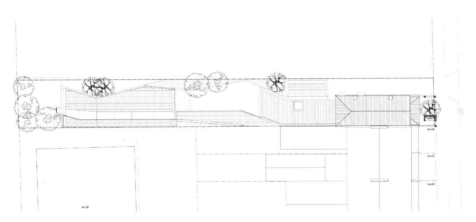

Roof plan

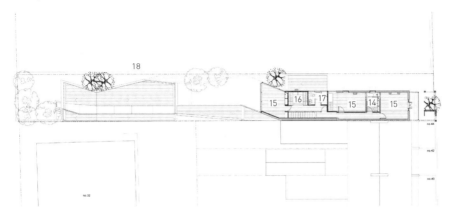

Second floor plan

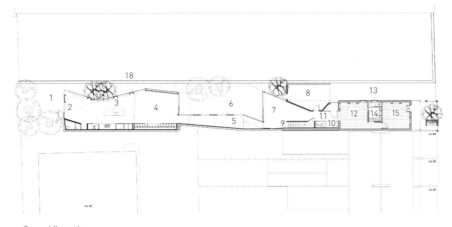

Ground floor plan

1. Courtyard
2. Dining
3. Kitchen
4. Living
5. Loggia
6. Lawn courtyard
7. TV room
8. Garage
9. Storage
10. Laundry
11. Entry
12. Study
13. Permeable driveway
14. Bathroom
15. Bedroom
16. Dressing room
17. En suite
18. Existing heritage brick wall

Spaces contract and expand: a large glazed room channels the circulation through a tall and narrow passage, which in turn, funnels it into another large room. This configuration creates a dynamic spatial experience enhanced by the natural light filtering through the glazed surfaces.

SLIM HOUSE

ALMA-NAC COLLABORATIVE ARCHITECTURE
LONDON, UNITED KINGDOM
© RICHARD CHIVERS

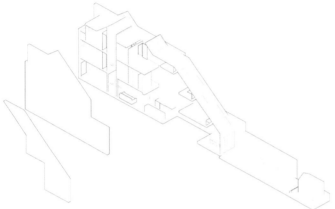

Exploded axonometric

Who would guess that this bright London townhouse was once a dark building with limited access to the garden? At just 7½ feet, its width was a challenge when it came to remodeling and expanding the house. Yet coupled with the restricted budget, these challenges led to a series of original and practical solutions.

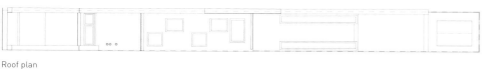

Roof plan

Third floor plan

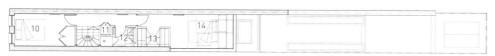

Second floor plan

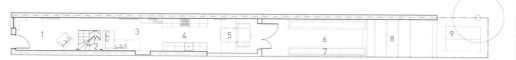

Ground floor plan

1. Entrance lounge
2. Stair
3. Living room
4. Kitchen
5. Dining
6. Garden
7. Planter
8. Deck / Pergola
9. Shed
10. Bedroom
11. Utility / Boiler
12. Bathroom
13. Dressing room
14. Master bedroom
15. Bedroom
16. Bathroom
17. Study / Spare room
18. Loft space

The narrow townhouse is located in a former stable access between two properties, which prevents the sidewalls from admitting natural light into the house. The project consists of a rear extension with a sloping roof to resolve the lighting problem.

This space is configured as a perfect breakfast area: a multipurpose space in which to eat, work, or read with good light and pleasant views.

Despite the challenge that the narrowness of the house presented, the upper floors were designed to accommodate new bathrooms that feel as spacious as they are functional.

The main goal was to bring light into the house through a sloping roof punctuated with skylights in order to create rooms on each level that feel spacious and bright.

OGIKUBO HOUSE

KIYOTOSHI MORI, NATSUKO KAWAMURA/MDS
TOKYO, JAPAN
© NORIYUKI YANO

With high land prices in Tokyo and strict laws that regulate construction in small places, designing a house to make the most of the available space can be a challenge. However, planning this house was a stimulating task: the aim was not to design another hermetically sealed structure, but to create a space in which the interior and exterior would communicate in perfect harmony.

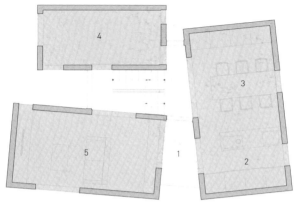

Second floor plan

1. Terrace
2. Kitchen
3. Dining
4. Bedroom
5. Living

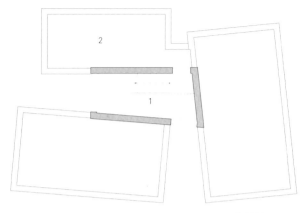

Roof plan

1. Void
2. Roof terrace

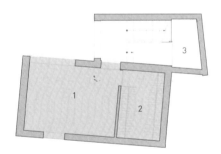

Basement floor plan

1. Bedroom
2. Walk-in closet
3. Storage

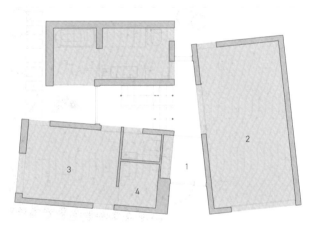

Ground floor plan

1. Entrance
2. Garage
3. Bedroom
4. Storage

This site is in a large, green, quiet residential area. To minimize any feeling of oppressiveness that a dense urban environment can produce, the house is formed by three separate blocks organized around a central light-filled staircase, creating courtyards.

The concept of "ma"—interval, pause, or gap—is a basic principle of the Japanese understanding of space. It is this that creates the feeling of openness and freedom.

As a result of this fragmentized layout, all the rooms of the house seem to spill out into the courtyards, producing an open feel. The design also focuses on establishing visual connections between the rooms contained in the different blocks and creating a dialogue between interior and exterior spaces.

The open character of the house enhances the spatial experience, offering constantly changing views that come with the passing of the seasons.

ELM COURT

MIKE FORD/AR DESIGN STUDIO
LONDON, UNITED KINGDOM
© MARTIN GARDNER

A dark and gloomy house in North London was transformed into a light-filled and airy home. The brief called for a single-story addition with minor alterations to the existing house. While the street facade retains its original appearance, the rear of the property is open to the garden.

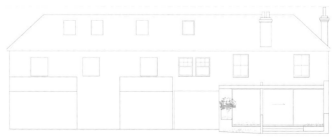

South elevation

The addition changed the atmosphere of the house. This was achieved by creating a new open plan living area facing the garden, optimizing functionality and improving the circulation between the different rooms and between the interior and the exterior.

Second floor plan

Ground floor plan

1. Dining
2. Reading
3. Patio
4. Outdoor dining
5. Relaxing
6. Kitchen
7. Toilet
8. Utility
9. Family room /
   Entertainment
   center
10. Bathroom
11. En suite
12. Master
    bedroom
13. Bedroom
14. Bedroom
15. Study

The greenery of the garden complements the neutral color palette of the open-plan kitchen and living room, breathing life into the house.

A series of aligned short walls mark the main circulation axis, connecting the existing house, the addition, and the garden beyond. The walls also organize the open-plan addition, creating subtle separations between areas of different use.

VOILA HOUSE

FABIAN TAN
KUALA LUMPUR, MALAYSIA
© EIFFEL CHONG

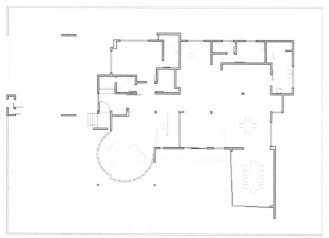

Ground floor plan

It is the umbrella trees in the garden that really catch one's attention when visiting this property. It is not surprising, therefore, that the transformation from gable-roofed bungalow into contemporary property has been structured around them. The common areas form a U-shape around the garden, while the kitchen and the bedrooms are on the opposite side.

A system of tall revolving screens is used to protect a circular living room from the sun. When the screens slide open, the living room transforms into a roofed open space with unobstructed views of the garden.

The location and size of the trees found in the garden guided the design of the house remodel. The trees were also used as shading devices to protect the exterior spaces.

An extended dining room frames the property along the side facing the neighboring homes, providing the garden with privacy and guiding views toward the circular living room.

The balanced and spacious common areas were designed with a white palette to allow natural light to spread throughout the space.

The design focuses on the reconfiguration of the ground floor. Alterations involved the tearing down of partitions to obtain open plan spaces. Little work was done on the upper floor, which was only extended to make the rooms larger.

The simple and accessory-free house interior favors the strong geometry of the building and the interrelation of spaces.

MIRANTE DO HORTO HOUSE

FLAVIO CASTRO
SÃO PAULO, BRAZIL
© NELSON KON

The premise behind this project was to maximize the size of the plot and volume of the house in order to optimize space. Specific areas were laid out around a vertical circulation, leaving the rest of the space as visible and flexible as possible. The result is a modern, dynamic, and ecologically sound home.

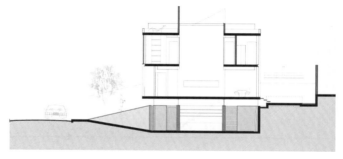

Section B

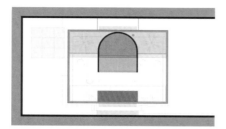

Roof plan

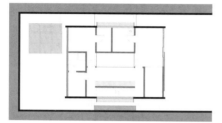

Upper floor plan

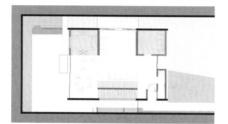

Main floor plan

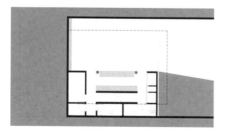

Garage level floor plan

Careful design and location of windows ensure minimal visual intrusion from and into the neighboring houses. Openings are maximized at the front and rear with a level of flexibility to control views and light.

The interior of the house is organized around a staircase and a full height void under a skylight. The latter brings abundant natural light into the house to compensate for the restrictions on window placement and size.

In this colorful and eclectic Bauhaus-inspired interior, everything, right down to the range hood, functions as a decorative element.

The social lives of this property's owners are busy, so a communal area was designed without clear limits, achieving a large, social space in which to enjoy meetings.

THE SNAKE

STEPHANE RASSELET, MARC-ANDRE PLASSE,
AMELIE MELAVEN/NATUREHUMAINE
MONTREAL, CANADA
© ADRIEN WILLIAMS

With the owners expecting twins, more space was required in this property. As the upper floors were tenanted, the expansion needed to be horizontal rather than vertical. The solution was to create an annex to the rear, which would house four bedrooms. Nicknamed "The Snake," the building rises from a base of red bricks that were reclaimed from the old garage.

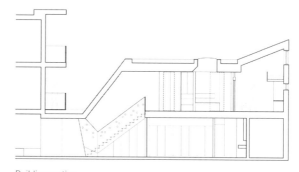

Building section

An orange guardrail with punched holes marks the transition to a playful area: the children's zone. This guardrail is a recurring design element that can be found in the form of a bed rail fence.

Playful design elements such as sliding window shutters, bunk beds, and brightly colored furnishings combined with plain plywood surfaces constitute the design language of the spaces, where kids surely would want to spend time in.

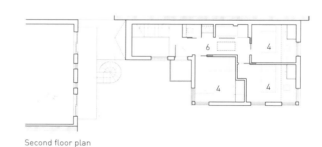

Second floor plan

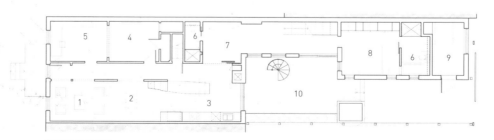

Ground floor plan

1. Living area
2. Dining area
3. Kitchen
4. Bedroom
5. Office
6. Bathroom
7. Game room
8. Master bedroom
9. Storage
10. Terrace

CLOISTER

02 ARCHITECTES
BRUSSELS, BELGIUM
© FILIP DUJARDIN

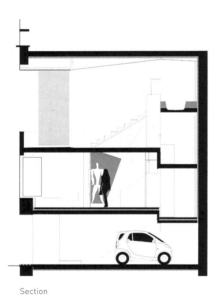

Section

The renovation of this Brussels house achieved four main objectives: to resolve problems of dampness, increase light, maximize the living area, and create a piece of unique architecture. With a black facade and pure white interior, this oasis of calm makes you forget you are in the heart of the city.

Despite the coldness of the white and the sobriety of the black, the fireplace and the brick buildings visible through the window bring a feeling of warmth and softness to the living room.

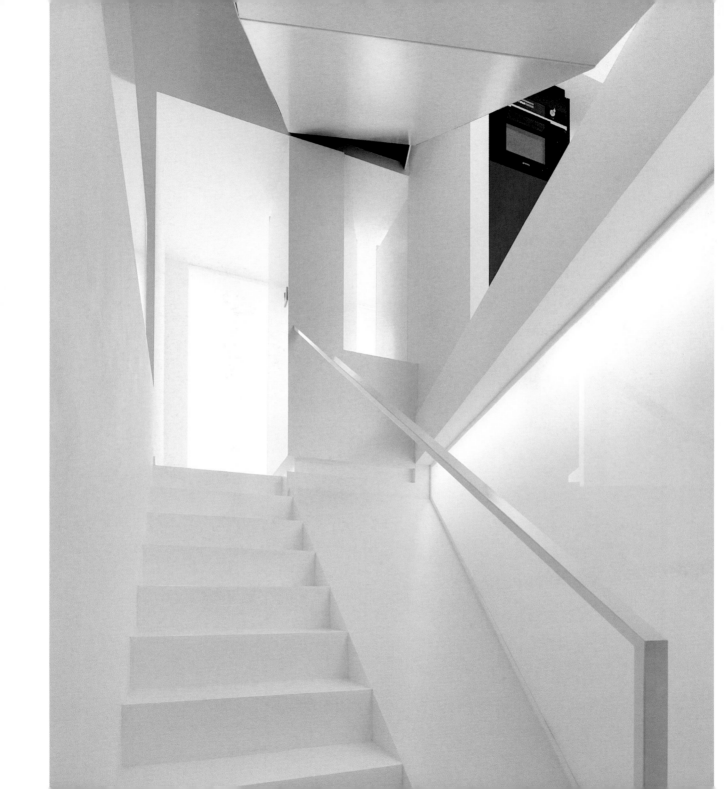

Minimal splashes of color disrupt the immaculate whiteness of the home: The fuchsia wall adds sensuality to a passage that leads to the private areas, while the black staircase with steel handrail adds a touch of sophistication with sharp detailing.

The aim was to create a fluid interior, enhanced by diagonals and a mostly white palette. Indeed, it seems that each element seamlessly merges into the next.

HOUSE IN RIMINI

**GIANCARLO GHIRARDELLI, DELPHINE CHOUAIB,
MARIO LA MATTINA/GHIRARDELLI ARCHITETTI**
RIMINI, ITALY
© VALENTINA BOVE

A new architectural body is added to this understated 1960s house: a curved metal roof with a serious yet contemporary feel. Inside, the steel frame that supports the attic structure adds an industrial flavor to daily life, while the windows link the house to the outside.

Front elevation

When combined with the concrete topping, the ribs of the steel deck provide the floor with additional hardness and strength. Left exposed, the ribbed steel deck adds to the aesthetic value of the space that it's used in.

The deck floor is made of composite steel, a strong but lightweight material compared to the cast-in-place concrete slab.

Attic floor plan

Second floor plan

1. Bedroom
2. Bathroom
3. Laundry
4. Open space
5. Kitchen and
   dining room
6. Living room
7. Terrace

A few eye-catching, colorful pieces in some of the rooms are enough to break up the uniformity of the white. This bright orange basin brings the bathroom to life.

The space is dominated by white, creating a bright and serene environment, notable for its clean lines and simple forms.

SMITH-CLEMENTI RESIDENCE

RIOS CLEMENTI HALE STUDIOS
VENICE, CALIFORNIA
© UNDINE PRÖHL

This property dating from 1920 was extended and renovated: a second piece of land was added, the common and private areas were reconfigured, and a new garage and suite were constructed. Refined cladding covers the front section, in memory of its bungalow origins, while the rear section boasts a striking wooden frame which provides shade to the master bedroom.

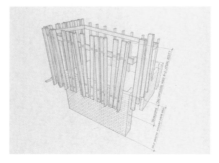

Perspective view of wooden frame

The main body of the house has varying rooflines and clerestory windows that express the changing levels and open the interior to the garden. The back volume contains the garage and the master bedroom above, with raw-wood framing around it, suggesting a tree house.

In the interior, materials were chosen to express functionality. Natural wood and plywood are used extensively, while allowing artwork and richly patterned accessories to add color and character.

The porch begins a black concrete-tile flooring that extends from outside through the first-floor living, dining, and kitchen areas, then back outside to the al fresco dining platform.

Upstairs, the family room is an open space and hub of activity. Materiality is further explored, always in line with the natural theme that ties the construction with the garden. The flooring changes from wood to cork tiles beyond an olive-colored floor-to-ceiling door that opens to the master bedroom.

A 7-foot-high plywood wall acts as a headboard, providing privacy, while the CMU wall extends up from the garage below and then through the full-height glass wall to the outdoor balcony.

The master suite, which includes a seating area, terrace, bath, and walk-in closets, has a hanging fireplace that swivels to direct heat either toward the balcony or the room.

Open shelves allow a visual connection between the master bedroom and the bathroom. They can alternately be closed off by sliding a red door all the way across.

SHERWOOD

TIM DORRINGTON/BOX LIVING
AUCKLAND, NEW ZEALAND
© EMMA-JANE HETHERINGTON

This project involved adding an extension to the rear of a New Zealand country house. The old house was restored to its original form and contains the nighttime areas (bedrooms and bathrooms). The two-story extension is a wood and glass box, accommodating the new living areas. Due to the slope of the site, the mezzanine lounge in the extension is directly linked to the original single-story house.

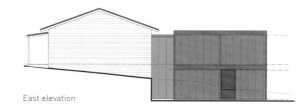

East elevation

The new extension, which houses the kitchen, living room, and dining room, is a double-height space, with the mezzanine suspended above the verdant garden.

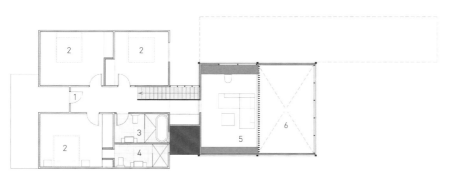

Entry level floor plan

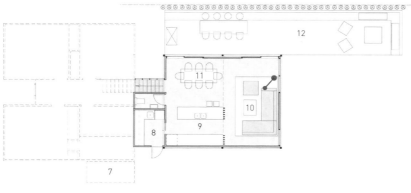

Ground floor plan

1. Entry
2. Bedroom
3. Bathroom
4. En suite
5. Mezzanine –
   Lounge
6. Void
7. Shed
8. Pantry
9. Kitchen
10. Lounge
11. Dining
12. Deck

The contemporary feel of the new extension is without doubt a contrast to the existing house. There is a clear difference between shapes, materials, and colors.

The extension has direct access to the backyard, one story below street level, where the original house is built. Some excavation work was required in order to align the original house's floor with that of the new mezzanine in the extension.

The design of the extension is guided by the desire to maximize the views to the backyard. Per structural reasons, the lower floor's back wall has a shear wall, but tension bracing was the design solution for the upper level to allow unobstructed views.

TOWNHOUSE

ELDING OSCARSON
LANDSKRONA, SWEDEN
© ÅKE E:SON LINDMAN

Encased in a row of period buildings, the house, with its smooth, white facade, is an oasis of contemporary beauty. Although the contrast is strong, the straight lines and simplicity of the white exterior enrich the rhythm of the street. The property is to be used as an art gallery, so the walls are designed not for privacy but for the display of paintings.

Cutaway building diagram

Site plan

Second floor plan

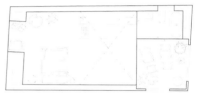

Mezzanine floor plan

Ground floor plan

Despite its reduced dimensions, the house is spacious and airy—mainly thanks to the staggered floors—while offering different spatial experiences, involving interior and exterior connections, long horizontal and vertical sightlines, and carefully framed views of the site.

The new house and separate home office occupy a narrow lot between old buildings. The design approach responds to the streetscape, which is defined by buildings of various periods, height, size, and facade material.

Open to the sky and the street, the interior is a juxtaposition of light and welcoming areas: the layout creates distinct corners here and there for reading and conversation.

An exposed metal deck and concrete floors, atypical ceiling heights, and a ground floor flush with the street level, were key elements that allowed three floors into a volume whose proportions are similar to those of some neighboring buildings.

Behind the row of buildings is a world of back-yards, brick walls, sheds, and vegetation. The project highlights this colorful environment by framing a courtyard between the house and the home office.

The sharp contrast between the new construction and its neighboring buildings is aimed at expressing inherent clarity and highlighting the beauty of the surroundings.

PLANALTO HOUSE

FLAVIO CASTRO
SÃO PAULO, BRAZIL
© NELSON KON

Conceived as an urban residence for a couple with two children, this house is a fine example of modern Brazilian architecture. It consists of two perpendicular buildings, which between them organize the different day-to-day functions: the private areas are located on the second floor in the rectangular prism, which sits perpendicular to the street, while the rest of the plot houses the communal and leisure areas.

Location map

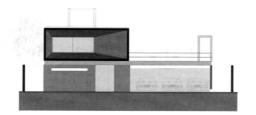

Front elevation

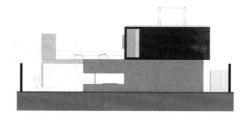

Back elevation

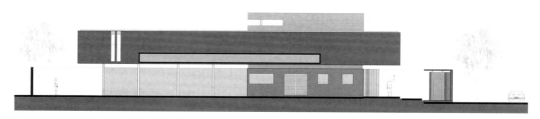

Right side elevation

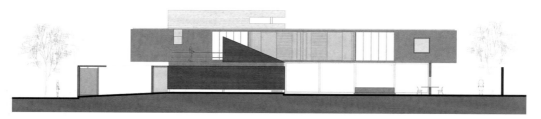

Left side elevation

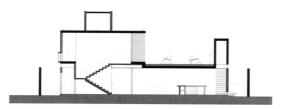

Section A

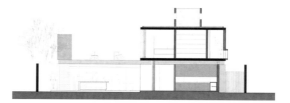

Section B

The roof next to the solarium is punctuated by three sculptural tubular skylights, which create a dramatic lighting effect at night, when lights are on in the recreation area below. A long skylight illuminates the garage adjacent to the recreation area.

The exterior opens up completely to the city of São Paulo, Brazil, becoming a little urban paradise: a place to indulge in the city from the tranquillity of the garden.

Concrete beams and steel columns are key elements of the architectural language, aimed at revealing the structural system of the house. Frameless floor-to-ceiling pivot doors are part of the design solutions to leave the structure as exposed as possible.

The concrete wall provides great privacy to this area of the house, while still enabling light to enter via a glass strip at the bottom.

HOMEMADE

BUREAU DE CHANGE DESIGN OFFICE
LONDON, UNITED KINGDOM
© ELIOT POSTMA

This project involved bringing together two adjoining properties as a single family home: the divisions between the two
houses were removed, new openings were created and, most
importantly, a heart was found for the new home. This was
achieved by creating a lined oak box that sits right in the center of the space, from which the staircase leading to the upper
floors departs.

House addition diagrams

A kitchen, dining, and open plan living area was created at the rear of the property, which opens to the outside via large patio doors.

The new kitchen seems to slide out from underneath the brick building, jutting out toward the garden. The contrast between old and new is visible from the outside and also from the interior, where exposed brick walls coexist with a polished resin floor and skylights lining the edge of the kitchen.

Ground floor plan

Integrating the bathroom into the bedroom space creates an area of relaxation and wellbeing. The elegant sunken bath functions as a piece of furniture in its own right.

This is a home that celebrates contrast, where new and old and light and dark combine to create interiors that are full of character.

MARACANÃ HOUSE

TERRA E TUMA ARQUITETOS ASSOCIADOS
SÃO PAULO, BRAZIL
© PEDRO KOK

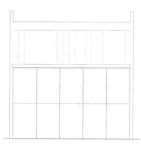

North elevation

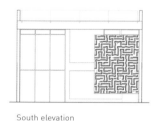

South elevation

Immersed in the urban environment of São Paulo, this home stands out among the red roofs of the Lapa district. Inside, the house is revealed as a playful area that is ruled by shape and color. The green of the plants plays an important role, percolating through the large glazed areas from the patios in which they are set.

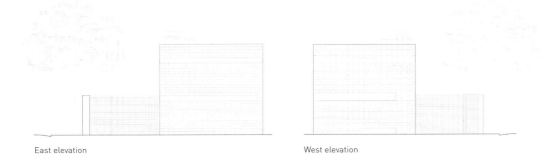

East elevation   West elevation

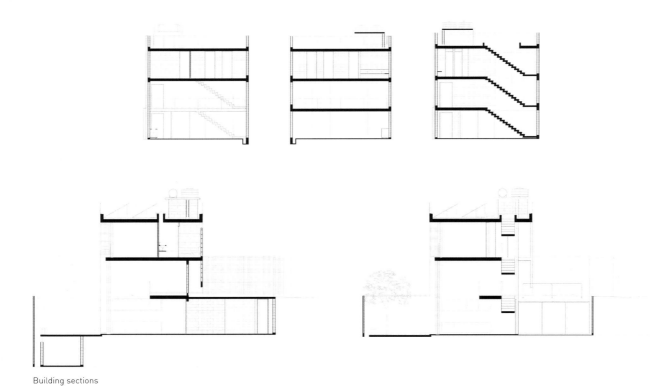

Building sections

The exposed concrete block walls lend the house an unmistakably industrial feel, unifying the interior and exterior.

The property was fully developed with the idea to create a sense of continuous space that includes both the exterior and the interior.

The challenge presented by the limitations of a narrow lot led to the creation of an indoor-outdoor house made possible with full height sliding glass doors and an interior courtyard framed along one side by a concrete staircase open to the sky above.

Although this is an open-plan living area, the space is configured to create more organized spaces, ideal for work or study.

HARRIS RESIDENCE

DIVISION1 ARCHITECTS
WASHINGTON, D.C.
© DEBI FOX PHOTOGRAPHY

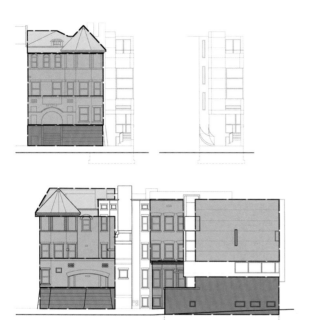

Elevations – Contextual study

This house was completely renovated from top to bottom. The brick and stucco facade makes it stand out from the neighboring houses and provides privacy to the interior, and the asymmetrical windows add a syncopated rhythm to the building. The new design is not intended to emulate the Victorian architecture that predominates in the neighborhood, but to introduce a palette of new materials that give the house its contemporary voice.

The remodel of the house explores the design opportunities that an original structure can offer. It creates a relationship that clearly separates old and new, while at the same time generating a connection between them.

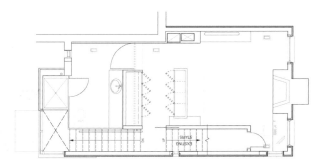

Third floor plan

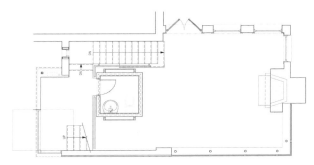

Second floor plan

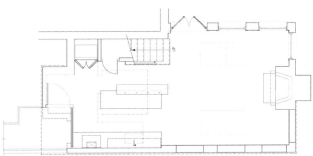

Ground floor plan

The design concept involves the addition of distinct elements around two sides of the building, and into its interior. While very dramatic, the design strategy is nonetheless very respectful toward the identity of the original building.

The inserted architectural elements slide neatly and precisely into the voids left inside the house. Their unexpected presence is enhanced by the use of materials and shapes that stand out radically within the container.

The predominance of black combined with straight lines creates a simple yet elegant space: a very contemporary bathroom with a minimalist feel.

HIDDEN HOUSE

TEATUM + TEATUM
LONDON, UNITED KINGDOM
© LYNDON DOUGLAS

Section through site

As its name suggests, this city-center house is a real hide-away. Its intimate architecture creates a transition between the public world and the private. The house makes an opportunity of its dislocation from the street by avoiding views of the exterior, enhancing a sense of interior space and focusing on light and materiality.

Second floor plan

Ground floor plan

1. Kitchen / Living
2. Living
3. Study (Under stairs)
4. Entry
5. Bathroom

6. Bedroom
7. Light well
8. Bedroom
9. Entry

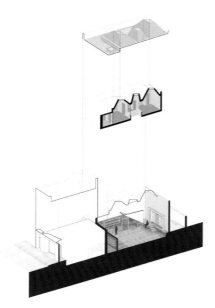

Exploded axonometric

The steel butterfly doors are laser cut to reflect the pattern of rain on a cold window. The pattern allows shards of light to filter into the spaces of the ground floor, while at the same time offering a visual texture that is perceived as artwork.

The lighting effects on materials and space are fully explored with results that are overpowering in a way that might remind one of the light installations by artist James Turrell.

CORTEN HOUSE

MARCIO KOGAN/STUDIO MK27
SÃO PAULO, BRAZIL
© NELSON KON

This house, which is located close to the largest park in São Paulo, is as surprising on the outside as it is extraordinary inside. The ornate facade, which rises behind the wooden garage door, is made from Corten steel. From the street the house appears compact and impenetrable: a private haven in one of the most populated cities in the world.

Location map

The site, long and narrow, is maximized with a three-story house and a small rear patio. An additional exterior space is found on the roof of the house, where users can enjoy views of the city.

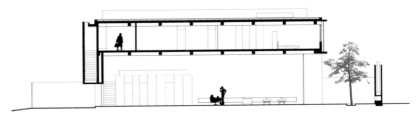

Longitudinal section

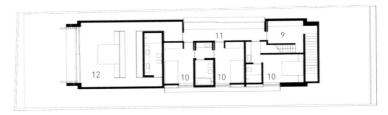

Third floor plan

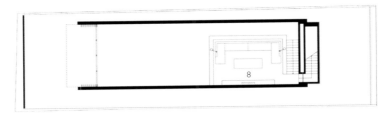

Second floor plan

Ground floor plan

1. Living room
2. Dining room
3. Kitchen
4. Maid's room
5. Pantry
6. Laundry
7. Patio
8. TV room
9. Family room
10. Bedroom
11. Office
12. Master bedroom

The front of the house stands out for its Corten steel cladding above the ground floor and garage door made of vertical wooden strips. The dialogue between the rust-colored finish and the wood, stone, white concrete, and glass surfaces constitute the architectural language of the house.

The rear patio and the living area can be perceived as separate spaces or as areas that com-
plement each other, so much so that the rear patio is an outdoor extension of the living area.

Taking advantage of the high ceiling on the ground floor, the living room contains a wooden volume that accommodates the kitchen and utilities program. Along the side closest to the entrance, a staircase leads to the mezzanine, which functions as a home theater.

From the mezzanine, another staircase gives way to the third floor containing the private program of the house, which in turn, has access to the roof terrace.

The climb up to the roof terrace is marked by a striking hatch with circular windows that slides sideways, opening the interior to the sky above. The hatch is finished in a material that echoes the Corten steel front facade.

The roof, with its heated pool set in a wooden deck, becomes an amazing viewpoint from which to enjoy the São Paulo skyline.

SOUTH PERTH HOUSE

MATTHEWS MCDONALD ARCHITECTS
PERTH, AUSTRALIA
© ROBERT FRITH/ACORN PHOTO

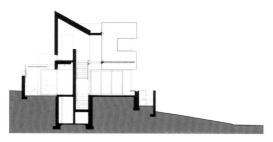

Section X

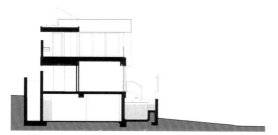

Section Y

The owners had lived in this house for many years but it was poorly planned and suffered from serious construction defects, so they decided to demolish it and build a new family home. The new house leverages the relationship between inside and out, and all rooms feature views to the Swan River and the city of Perth.

The massing of the house has been broken down into smaller parts. Different materials are used to articulate these parts, while adding visual texture. In that respect, masonry walls create a podium and backbone for the steel and glass volumes.

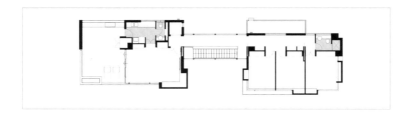

Second floor plan

Ground floor plan

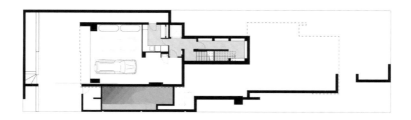

Basement floor plan

In contrast to the traditional houses of suburban Australia, this property is formed around a courtyard with a gallery linking the two parts of the building.

A pool extends parallel to the facade. Hidden from the street behind a low wall, it reveals itself as a place for secret enjoyment.

The client's interest in cooking and entertaining has driven the design, which provides a flexible layout. As a result, special consideration was given to the way the home will be used.

The bathtub is the perfect place in which to relax and be soothed by beautiful views of the Perth skyline.

SENTOSA HOUSE

NICHOLAS BURNS
SENTOSA, SINGAPORE
© PATRICK BINGHAM-HALL

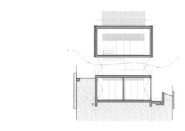

Cross section

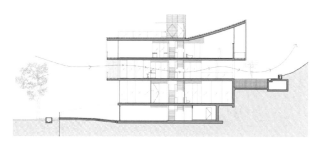

Longitudinal section

This house on the island of Sentosa is designed to adapt to a wide variety of uses and remain impervious to the rapid changes of the island. Wide-open, interactive, flexible spaces await behind a facade with large windows and balconies. The space is configured to make the most of the views while maximizing privacy.

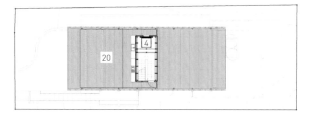

Roof terrace floor plan

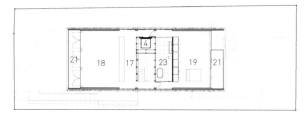

Fourth floor plan

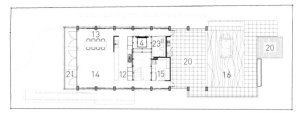

Third floor plan

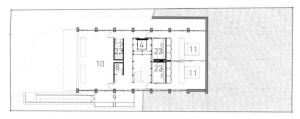

Second floor plan

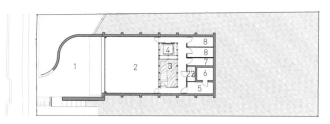

Ground floor plan

1. Driveway	13. Dining
2. Garage	14. Living
3. Reflection pond	15. Laundry
4. Elevator	16. Pool
5. Plant	17. Study
6. Cellar	18. Lounge
7. Pool plant	19. Master bedroom
8. Storage	20. Terrace
9. Entrance	21. Balcony
10. Gallery	22. Powder room
11. Bedroom	23. Bathroom
12. Kitchen	

Teak wood, concrete, steel, and glass provide the base materials for the interior. Every detail exudes warmth and modernity in this design.

A series of open spaces are clustered against a core that provides structure and vertical circulation, as well as space for bathrooms and service rooms.

The structural grid provides a coherent house plan. Every element and detail relates to and relies on different scales, while materials are chosen for the expressive power of their natural beauty.

The kitchen offsets the core. Its compact and simple design optimizes space and merges with the open plan living area, becoming a focus during entertaining events.

MEASER RESIDENCE

DK DESIGNHOUSE
VENICE, CALIFORNIA
© JOHN ELLIS

When the owner of this property decided to renovate it, he didn't imagine that the designer in charge of the lighting would end up sharing it as his wife. A series of vertical panels at the front obscure the sunlight and provide privacy to the interiors, while the glass surfaces allow the light to filter in.

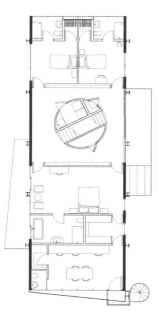

Second floor plan

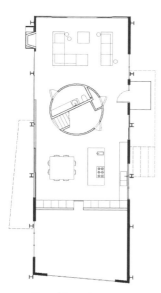

Ground floor plan

With its standing-seam siding and large windows, the building looks like two elegant shipping containers stacked one on top of the other. Surrounded by a low concrete wall and set close to the property line, the house is conspicuously open to the street.

The ground floor is freed from interior barriers, foregoing boxy rooms with designated functions. Instead, it is a single large room that encompasses a free-flowing kitchen, dining, and living areas.

The living area, at one end of the ground floor, is virtually open to the garden on all three sides, only framed by two facing walls—one integrating a fireplace—to demarcate the rectangular shape of the house.

A large cylinder occupies a prominent place in the layout of the house, spanning both floors. Its central position allows for the creation of areas with specific, designated functions, avoiding the need of partitions.

The open-plan kitchen-dining room is located on one side of the cylindrical structure. Colored stools and chairs add a playful touch to the room.

A staircase slices the cylindrical structure. This design gesture is further enhanced by the bright orange color applied to the walls supporting the stairs. On the ground floor, the cylinder also contains a powder room, closet, and pantry; on the second floor, it conceals another closet and audio system.

The interiors of the second floor respond to a traditional home layout, with rooms clearly demar-
cated by walls, and reflect the owner's initial in-
spiration for building the home.

The second floor's design, which focuses on providing privacy and comfort, contrasts with the casual and playful plan of the ground floor. However, they both take full advantage of natural light filtering through large glazed surfaces along the perimeter of the house.

CHURCH STREET RESIDENCE

DIVISION1 ARCHITECTS
WASHINGTON, D.C.
© DEBI FOX PHOTOGRAPHY

The interior of this twentieth century townhouse, which was fragmented into several rooms, has been transformed into an agreeable and highly flexible open-plan space. The new home is spacious and full of light, boasting sophisticated technological solutions that qualify it as an environmentally sustainable home with passive ventilation and water recycling systems.

Cutaway diagram of the townhouse

The interior of the existing house was entirely gutted to accommodate the new program, which includes two separate dwellings. One occupies the ground floor and has access to a rear patio, the other spans over two levels and has access to a roof terrace.

The dining area and the kitchen of the upper dwelling occupy a double height space, which makes up for the long and narrow proportions of the interior.

Here, every detail reinforces the idea of aesthetic minimalism: open space, straight lines, abundant light, and reflective white.

A series of architectural elements appear to slide through the space vertically and horizontally, encouraging a sense of movement.

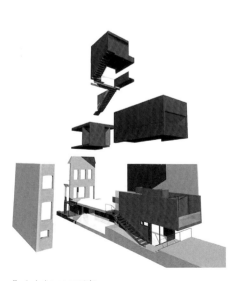

Exploded axonometric

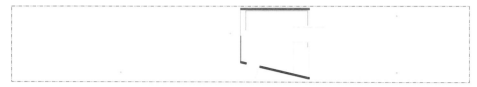

Roof terrace plan

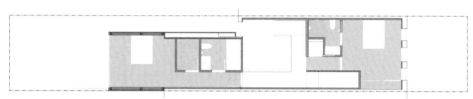

Third floor plan

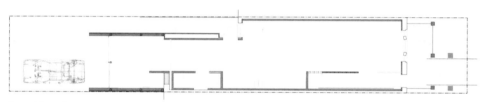

Second floor plan

Ground floor plan

Far from being dull, the limited color and material palette enhances the play of light on the different surfaces, enhancing the spatial experience.
Materials were chosen to mark a clear distinction
between old and new.

HOUSE IN MEGUROHONCHO

TORAFU ARCHITECTS
TOKYO, JAPAN
© TORAFU ARCHITECTS

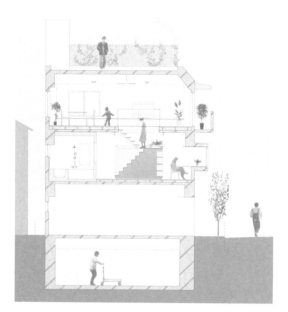

Building section

The first part of a two-phase project for the refurbishment of a forty-year-old, mixed-use, reinforced concrete building, involves the design of the building's exterior and the apartments on its second and third floors. Towering above the surrounding houses, the third floor accommodates well-lit living areas, while the second floor offers more private spaces.

A large wooden element is located directly below an opening made in the third floor slab. It is conceived as a multifunctional item that blurs the boundaries between architecture and furniture.

Other than the freestanding piece of furniture, the new elements are fully integrated into the existing space. In that respect, the long bay window on the second floor is turned into a built-in desk.

The top of the wooden element is short of the second floor's ceiling and right underneath the opening in the third floor. This design gesture addresses the notion of an inserted object into an existing space.

The third floor, accommodating the living areas, is well lit and benefits from long views of the city above the neighboring rooftops, compared to the significantly more private nature of the second floor where the bedrooms are located.

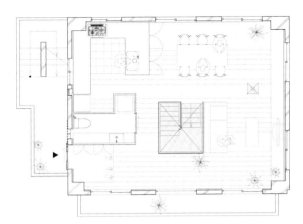

Third floor plan

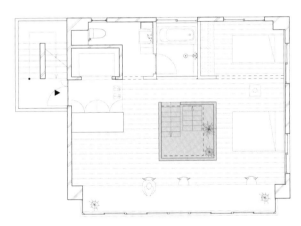

Second floor plan

This freestanding piece of furniture, incorporating storage space and the first flight of stairs leading to the third floor, organizes the second floor open plan, creating separate areas of different functions.

The top of the freestanding furniture is a wide landing, where a second flight of stairs starts. While the first flight seems to be carved into the wooden furniture, the second has open risers, emphasizing the separation between the piece of furniture and the architecture.

MEJIRO HOUSE

KIYOTOSHI MORI, NATSUKO KAWAMURA/MDS
TOKYO, JAPAN
© TOSHIYUKI YANO

In the densely populated center of Tokyo, households tend to turn in on themselves, avoiding street views and hiding behind high walls to maximize privacy. To avoid this feeling of claustrophobia, the house was orientated to maintain its connection with the outside world, creating a bright and breezy interior that nonetheless preserves its privacy.

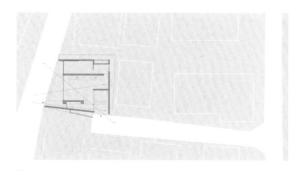

Site plan

Second floor plan

1. Bedroom
2. Void

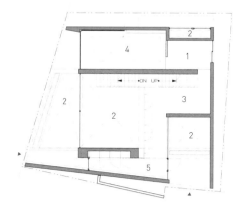

Building section

1. Garden
2. Living
3. Garden
4. Gallery
5. Bedroom

Basement floor plan

1. Garden
2. Living
3. Garden
4. Dining
5. Kitchen
6. Storage
7. Workroom

Ground floor plan

1. Entrance
2. Void
3. Gallery
4. Garage
5. Storage

Past the entry, the interior of the house opens up to a sunken courtyard that allows light into the spaces below street level, while giving them privacy, out of visual reach from passersby and neighboring houses.

All the spaces boast an open feel provided by the generous use of glass and white surfaces that reflect the light coming from the various courtyards that articulate the house.

The living room receives natural light from different angles: through the glass wall at one end, a courtyard at the opposite end, and a skylight above the staircase connecting the living room and the gallery spaces on the ground floor.

The living room is located in the basement that, paradoxically, is usually considered a dark and uninviting space. This issue was resolved by creating a double height living room that opens to a narrow courtyard framed by a tall concrete wall that rises past a sidewalk to shoulder height.

The white, gray, and black color palette and the textures of the cement, wood, and stone materials give this house a strong industrial feel.

Other than the entry, the ground floor only contains gallery spaces articulated by voids created by the courtyards. This level acts as a middle ground between the urban environment and the home.

NOK SUNG HUN

HYOMAN KIM/IROJE KHM ARCHITECTS
SEONGNAM, SOUTH KOREA
© JONGOH KIM

The building's name literally means "the house that listens to the sound of nature and thinks of the future of life." Composed of two parts, a main residence and a guesthouse, the dwelling has all the benefits of city convenience and embraces the smells and sounds of the natural landscape where it's set. Its complex roofline reflects the disparate urban architecture.

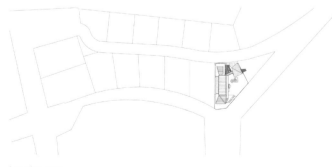

Location map

Front elevation

Left elevation

Rear elevation

Right elevation

Throughout the garden, in the space between the two buildings, a series of sculptural elements frame the different views of the house.

The zinc and wood-paneled internal partitions of the house confer on the space a feeling of being semi-open to the elements.

By using the same materials inside and out, the separation between the two spaces has been blurred. The smells of the surrounding landscape are almost palpable from within the house itself.

The interior of the house is spacious and feels airy thanks to the large windows and cutouts in the partitions, letting abundant light reach all corners of the house.

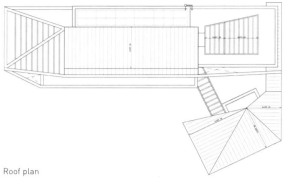

Roof plan

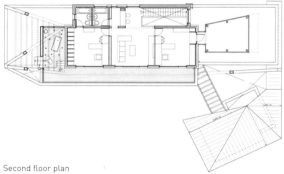

Second floor plan

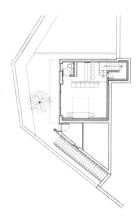

Basement floor plan

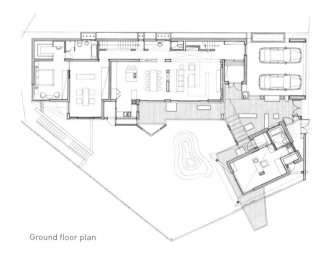

Ground floor plan

The design of the house fully explores the connection between interior and exterior through the creation of courtyards, which articulate different parts of the house and bring light into the interior.

The angled roof is one of the most prominent features of the house, giving the building a strong identity. Conceptually, the profile of the house echoes the mountains rising in the horizon.